I AM ALL OF THOSE PEOPLE

By Diane Sharp

I Am All of Those People
Trilogy Christian Publishers A Wholly Owned Subsidiary of Trinity Broadcasting Network
2442 Michelle Drive Tustin, CA 92780
Copyright © 2023 by Diane Sharp
All Scripture quotations are taken from the ESV® Bible (The Holy Bible, English Standard Version®), copyright © 2001 by Crossway Bibles, a publishing ministry of Good News Publishers. Used by permission. All rights reserved.
No part of this book may be reproduced, stored in a retrieval system, or transmitted by any means without written permission from the author. All rights reserved. Printed in the USA.
Rights Department, 2442 Michelle Drive, Tustin, CA 92780.
Trilogy Christian Publishing/TBN and colophon are trademarks of Trinity Broadcasting Network.
Cover design by: Trilogy
For information about special discounts for bulk purchases, please contact Trilogy Christian Publishing.
Trilogy Disclaimer: The views and content expressed in this book are those of the author and may not necessarily reflect the views and doctrine of Trilogy Christian Publishing or the Trinity Broadcasting Network.
Manufactured in the United States of America
10 9 8 7 6 5 4 3 2 1
Library of Congress Cataloging-in-Publication Data is available.
ISBN: 979-8-88738-503-7
E-ISBN: 979-8-88738-504-4

To the only wise God

TABLE OF CONTENTS

Acknowledgments. 7

Chapter 1. 9

Chapter 2. 25

Chapter 3. 39

Chapter 4. 45

Chapter 5. 51

Chapter 6. 73

Chapter 7. 101

Chapter 8. 103

Chapter 9. 105

Reconciliation Calls to Action 107

Endnotes 109

ACKNOWLEDGMENTS

Thank you to all of my friends and family who had to hear about "the book" for years, and none of you were annoyed. To Dr. Steven Crowther, friend and mentor, who is now with our Savior but, while he was here, encouraged me to finish this book by telling me, "Don't let what you think it should look like stop you from doing it." Well, Dr. Crowther—here it is.

To Terry Munday, whose accountability in the form of frequent "How is the book coming?" emails kept this project alive. To Raymond L. Balogh Jr., whose tireless editing shaped this into something worth reading. Thank you for being excited with me.

To my father, K. D. Sharp, who made books important to me as a child, read with me before bed every night, and drove me on demand to the library entirely too often when I knew he was tired.

And to my children and grandchildren, Van, Tashi, Mia, Chantal, Elijah, and Ezra. May this book and my life leave a legacy beyond what I could ever deserve.

—Dr. Diane Sharp

CHAPTER 1

Terry should wear a suit more often. I am impressed with my older brother's transformation from the tormentor who gave me charley horses while I slept to impress all the girls at my slumber party to a real man who actually looks pretty nice under the blinding lights of the church stage.

It could just be the subject matter of his speech that makes him shine; he's saying nice things about me. He looks a bit uncomfortable behind a pulpit (somewhere none of us would ever expect he would end up) and probably more uncomfortable talking about emotions, especially in front of a group. The occasional tug at his collar and tie reminds everyone he's more used to wearing fatigues during the day and ratty jeans during his off time.

Looking around the room, I see friends from elementary through high school whom I haven't seen in years. I see family, some of whom lived close by and some from out

I Am All of Those People

of state. I see new and old friends and some coworkers. It feels good to know they're here to celebrate me.

I want to spend time telling each one of them how much I love them all.

But I can't. I'm dead.

It's an intensely surreal experience attending your own funeral. I'm not sure how this is "allowed," but it feels nice, so I'm not going to question it. Nobody can see me or hear me. At least I assume they can't. I haven't tried to talk to anyone yet because talking would be rude at a funeral. But I do know they can't see me because they would simultaneously be seeing the other me lying in a box at the foot of the stage. And since no one is freaking out when they glance in my direction, I surmise I'm invisible.

A hiking accident ended my life at age fifty-two. My demise was unexpected but quick, with no lingering pain. Not a bad way to go—considering some of the other life choices I made throughout the years. I was adventurous to a fault. I traveled the world every chance I got, wanting to learn everything I could about new people groups. I'd travel just about anywhere time and money would allow and find where the locals went so I could get a real view of the countries and their people. Egypt was my favorite— no, it was Pakistan. That trip was crazy. I never told my dad what happened there when our mission team got

Dr. Diane Sharp

discovered by the local terrorists. He never understood why anyone would leave the US on purpose. I can still hear him say, "I went to Korea, and that was it for me!" In his opinion, everywhere that wasn't America amounted to wartime Korea. I doubt the word "cautious" will surface in any remembrance speeches today.

I'm sitting behind my Uncle Billy and Aunt Patricia. They look like politicians, dressed, as usual, in the sharpest suits without a hair out of place. But I secretly know that my Aunt has just enough free-spirit boho-hippie in her that she'd really rather be wearing something much more comfortable. They know a lot of really important people and frankly *are* really important people, so to see they traveled all the way here just to remember me is a pretty big honor.

Uncle Billy looks like he did when he got a medal from the president for his work in philanthropy: a tall, stoic Lakota man. She looks like the same dutiful wife and refined people-loving socialite who stood next to him in 1964 when he won a gold medal at the Tokyo Olympics. My people. I want to tap them on the shoulder and tell them, "Thanks for coming. Thanks for making me feel like I mattered." But I'll refrain, just to be safe. He taught me so much about generational trauma and generational privilege. And about how important it is to implement the often-overlooked element of social justice when making efforts to reach out and help people.

I wonder what I look like right now. Well, not "dead in the box" me. I can see that, but me here in this seat listening to my brother give a shockingly good speech about what it was like growing up with me. Um, did he just call me pesky?

"Molly," Terry continued, "had a deep love for nature where sometimes I thought I saw her talking to the trees. She loved to be outside anywhere near water, especially the beach. She said the ocean always reminded her of how small she and her problems were relative to the vastness of creation. Even though she was younger than me, I could never beat her in a footrace. She ran long-distance like no one I've ever met, and sometimes I thought she was going to go until parts fell off." The crowd chuckled.

"But the one trait I always wish I had was her generosity. I can't count the times we would be out somewhere, and if a cashier—or anyone, really—complimented something she had or a piece of her handmade jewelry she had on, she'd take it off and give it to them right there."

Actually, I stopped this when it came to earrings. I thought people would think it was gross to take something out of an actual hole in my body. Instead, I'd go home and make them their own and bring them back to their store later.

"Molly loved reading. Our dad built some shelves in my closet for my sporting equipment and clothes, but Molly

Dr. Diane Sharp

made him build bookshelves because she was running out of space in every available cranny in her bedroom. She would sit outside under the trees in our backyard and read until it got too dark to see. I always wished I were as smart as she was."

Whoa! He envied me? Back in school, he was the good-looking jock everyone wanted to be friends with. I was the flat-chested nerd with the giant front teeth and thick glasses so big my forehead could see clearly too. It's amazing the stuff you hear at your funeral.

I watch with deep compassion as Terry picks up his notes from the podium, wipes his eyes on his sleeve, and leaves the stage to return to his seat and into the arms of his wife. I want so much to run and give him a hug. I didn't dig his wife so much when I first met her, but I'm glad she's there to hold him for me now.

Next up on the podium are my girls, their copper skin and perfect makeup glowing under the stage lights. They are so beautiful, even more beautiful than I remembered. The highlight from their speech is the way I encouraged them to be kind and confident. Mia's perfect posture reminds me of how I taught them to "walk into a room like you own it, and no one will know that you don't."

My daughters are multiracial, which adds another level of challenge to doing life as a woman in this world. But they genuinely love all people and yearn to serve the hurting, and there is not one group of our people with whom they can't fit in. My son didn't speak for his own reasons of family fallout. But he came. *See*—I smile like a Cheshire cat—*you know you love me.*

The girls are talking about how I made rainy days so warm and cozy with my spaghetti you could smell from the front porch and what an amazing job I did raising them by myself. It's nice to hear them talk about some of the struggles I thought went unnoticed. I am so proud of who they are now. I'm fighting to convince myself they're going to be fine without me here to protect them. This planet can be a trip, but they are both so fiercely independent and smart.

"I remember Mom working on her degree in the living room she converted into an education war room with whiteboards covering every wall. My favorite was the one where she wrote out all the possible ways to help on the reservation. She'd stand there and write fervently and sometimes just stare at it in tears because there were too many things for her to do by herself, and she would wrestle to get clarity on what her role was even supposed to be."

I still have that whiteboard. Oh, wait, I don't have "stuff," not in my current condition.

"I still have that whiteboard," Mia says through slowly mounting tears.

Dr. Diane Sharp

Yessss. Fist bump.

On the seat next to me is a program open to my obituary. Curious to see what information made it in there, I read it to myself while I wait for the next speaker. Whoever is up next will be speaking via video, so the sound guy has to take a moment to cue it up.

The obit reads, "Molly died at the age of fifty-two, leaving behind her daughters, Mia and Tashi, and her son, Van."

I didn't *leave* them behind. Ugh, whoever wrote this thing acted like I did this on purpose! I can't stop editing people's horrible writing—even when I'm dead.

"She is preceded in death by her mother, Donna Doreen Sharp, and her father, K. D. Sharp."

Best. Parents. Ever. English and Irish in descent, quite a bit lighter in skin color than me (especially in the summer), but they were mine. They were my people.

"She received her doctorate in education with a focus on traumatology and taught at a number of Christian and Bible universities. Molly was a dean at Melton University in Fayetteville, North Carolina. Her desire was to use her education to help with suicide prevention and improve education systems serving Native American populations."

Trauma educated—Christian beliefs, White family, Native bloodline. I always pondered how that was the perfect setup to connect my diverse worlds and my people to one another and really make a difference in how we all see and treat each other. Too bad I never got the chance.

The video booms on with the sound entirely too loud. Folks grimace and turn their heads toward where the sound came from, but it is quickly adjusted, and none other than my best friend Stephanie takes to the screen.

"I don't do funerals. Molly knew that. But there is no way I can let her leave this earth without telling everyone how I feel about her."

I already know, my friend. We had the conversation more than once about what we'd say and whether or not we'd even be composed enough to attend each other's funerals, and I gave her permission to miss mine. I knew how she felt about death. As we sat in her Italian restaurant laughing until we couldn't see straight, we'd talk about which of our silly adventures we could share and which ones were best kept to ourselves. I made her promise to serve spaghetti at my funeral. I don't smell any, so maybe she didn't—or maybe I just can't smell now. I'll check it out afterward.

"Molly was always serving people. Always. Intentionally looking for ways to help. We were helping a recently divorced friend of hers set up a yard sale. That was no shocker. She was always volunteering me to help her help others, signing me up for stuff I didn't want to do. But secretly I loved the time we spent doing it. In the bargain box of fifty-cent yard sale items was a book called *Racing Jesus*. I bought the book without telling her and gave it to her later. That book summed up who Molly was."

Ew. Was. I'm "was" now.

"It was like she would race Jesus Himself to see who could get to hurting people faster. Her heart's desire was to make a change on the reservation where she was from, to make the world better for them. And not just there but everywhere. She wanted to leave this world better than she found it and every person better than she found them.

"She did that with me. Without going into too much detail, I had a very dark period in my life after experiencing the tragic loss of my husband. I don't remember much of anything that happened afterward, but in one moment of clarity, I remember Molly bringing food to our house. Wherever she was, you could be sure good food was somewhere close by. Back then I couldn't even muster up the strength to voice a 'thank you,' but I was so grateful. She sat next to me on the couch for a bit that day and just let me sit there and not speak.

"She knew how to love me in the most fun times and in the darkest hours of my life. It was with her that I laughed for the first time in years after my Mike died. I don't think we ever stopped laughing after that. We'd laugh until we'd cough uncontrollably with tears pouring down our cheeks. On more than one occasion, people around us would say, 'I want to be sitting at *that* table.' I was honored to be at any table or any event with my best friend. She was the event queen. She always said I was, but I argued it was her. Either way, if one of us had an event to run, the other was right there, working like a dog." Stephanie pauses for a moment, no doubt wistfully remembering one of our tandem labors of love.

"Molly genuinely loved her family and friends, who came from every walk of life. She'd always call them 'her people.' I am a full-blooded Cherokee, but it wasn't until after Molly got connected to her Lakota family and embraced her newfound heritage with so much reverence and excitement that I was able to appreciate and be proud of my own Indigenous heritage. I can't see y'all past these lights right now, but I guarantee there is someone in this gathering sitting close by your seat who doesn't look like you.

"Molly loved people from all walks of life, and they loved her too. She treated everyone the same. Sometimes she would introduce me to a person, and I'd wonder where in the world she would possibly have met this person. After talking to them for five minutes, I would see them for the gems all those people were. But Molly immediately saw the true beauty in everyone. We should all be like she was."

Will I ever get used to being referred to as "was"?

"Grief may cause you to long for Molly's presence, but don't worry. I'm going to tell you where you can find her. You'll find Molly wherever you hear laughter, and you'll find Molly wherever people are hurting because she refused to leave them in their pain." The mood in the room is shifting from tearful to encouraged. "And wherever you find spaghetti before 9 a.m. being washed down with a Pepsi…"

Stephanie's mouth is still moving on the screen, but suddenly I can't hear a word she's saying. There's a rising crescendo of chaos in the room, and people are springing up out of their seats, holding programs over their heads. Water is spraying everywhere! I can't feel a thing, but I recognize the problem—the fire sprinklers have been activated! One of the hospitality crew (fancy word for the building maintenance team) makes his way to the stage and grabs the microphone.

"There is no fire. I repeat, *no fire*. But please exit the room quickly. They were working on a pipe in the basement, and somehow the sprinkler system has been triggered. There are sensors in the sprinkler heads that will turn off once they no longer detect people in the room, so please leave your belongings and immediately head for the nearest exit so we can minimize the water damage."

Wait, I'm not getting wet. Not "ghostly invisible spy" me but "casket" me. The stage and my casket are bone dry. The sprinklers are only dousing the seating area, causing a flurried rush of people heading to the exits without their belongings. That coat check in the back of the room seems like less of a good idea now because the coat check girls are gone, making it impossible for anyone to get their coats and whatever contents are housed in the pockets.

Seriously? Seriously. Only at my funeral. Some of my less "religious" friends used to joke about the fire alarm going off if they would ever walk into church—and here we are. I imagine I should go out too. Nothing to see here until this mess is over. I follow the fast-moving river of people out the doors as the staff ushers everyone into the student center building next door.

I overhear a mixture of sentiments, "I can't believe this." "My phone is in there!" And those folks who thought no one was listening, "I would leave, but my keys are in my jacket." "I'm not leaving my purse. I'll stay until this is sorted out. I'm sure it won't be long."

A few are still shedding tears, but I guess the shock of being doused with chemical-laced water snapped most of the attendees out of their grief. Good night, I can't even die normally! Then there are my close friends who know I would want nothing more than for people to laugh it off and handle it with as much humor as they can muster. I make my way into the student center with the rest of the herd—and then it hits me. The sweet, rich, thyme-laced aroma of...*spaghetti*! She did it! Stephanie came through. Attagirl!

The sound system screeches with that noise you usually hear before an unplanned announcement. "Can I have everyone's attention, please? We cannot apologize enough for this. Again, no fire, just a sensor issue that should be taken care of very quickly. You should be able to reenter and collect your belongings very, very soon. But in the meanwhile, we will be opening up the brunch buffet early, so you can enjoy some food while you wait. Molly would want 'her people,' as she always said, to be served immediately."

Truth.

Laughter seems to prevail, and people collectively forgive the crisis and line up for some pasta. Spaghetti heals all. I tried to educate people on its power when I was—ugh, I'm calling myself "was" now.

The tables fill up with the people I love, and before long, barely any seats are left. Sitting in the worship center building during the funeral, I found it difficult to gauge how many people actually showed up to say their goodbyes, but now it's a standing room only in the student center! To know that so many people loved me in life and took the time to come to my funeral is humbling. And these are just the folks who could make it. You should see the flowers. They're everywhere! I prefer a donation to the university where I worked, but I guess I didn't make that desire clear when I was alive.

I'm enjoying the smell, but I'm not hungry—perhaps another side effect of my, um, current condition. I decide to read the notes on the flowers. Some of them (the cards and the flowers) are pretty sweet. A number of them contain the usual sympathy message, but some get personal.

"Molly meant so much to my family. She helped us find resources when my husband lost his job."

"Molly's laughter will be greatly missed at our events."

"She left this world better than she found it."

But did I? Like how? I mean—I always said I wanted to. Did I really?

I wonder if I can cry.

I watch as Uncle Billy and Aunt Pat make their way around the room. Throngs of people want pictures and autographs and to tell him what his Olympic victory meant to them. You'd think people would reel back their stargazing at a funeral.

They're also mingling with Steve, a United States senator, and his wife, Audrey. Steve and Audrey live in Montana, so I know they made quite a trek to be here in North Carolina. They do travel a lot, particularly to DC, for work, so maybe they combined this visit with another East Coast venture.

Kind of sounds like I traveled in important political circles. Nope. Steve's my cousin. I met him and his family at a reunion Aunt Patricia had invited me to shortly after we met. Steve taught me so much about the current political crises facing Indigenous people in the US.

Uncle Billy and Aunt Patricia were the first family members I met—birth family, that is. I was adopted six weeks after I was born by an amazing couple who have both died, my mom long before my dad. That explains why they're not here—or wait, maybe they are. After all, *I'm* here, soooo…I scan the room, but I don't see them, so I guess not. But I'm sure I'll run into them at some point in this convoluted afterlife system. I'm new to the whole *dead* thing, so I don't know how it all works.

I'm amazed at the diversity in the crowd, with literally people of every color and race I can think of. I'm reveling in the variety of heritages represented. And all of them are equally my people.

Out of the corner of my eye, I see a slow-moving trio. The woman in the middle is being held up on either side by two people I don't recognize. Oh my gosh, that's my birth mother! She looks like a tired version of the woman in the pictures I'd seen years earlier. She is weeping quietly while simultaneously buckling at the knees. The two people flanking her are helping her walk. Her face is red, her eyes swollen, as though she'd been crying for days. As she brushes past me, I can hear her quietly repeating, "I'm so sorry; I'm so sorry."

Sorry? For what? Doesn't she know she's the hero in my story? I want desperately to reach out and hold her face up and tell her, "Thank you. Thank you because you could have killed me when you found out you were pregnant, but you didn't. You let me live, knowing your life would never be the same and you were probably going to face some ridicule for having a baby and giving her up. I am here because of your bravery. Don't cry. I'm alive because of you." But she can't hear me.

****

CHAPTER 2

I got reconnected to my birth family in my early twenties by way of an absolute miracle chance meeting in a restaurant. Some people would call it coincidence; others would harken to their conscience. Some would say they just felt a burden. But I call it "God told me..."

God told me to quit the piece-of-cake job I had at a casino outside of Minneapolis, where I was making killer money to sling sodas (it was a dry casino, so no alcohol was allowed). I don't think I'd ever quit a job without having another one in the works, and I normally worked at least two jobs while I went to college. But I was obedient to the compulsion and resigned. I applied everywhere for a new job, and no one would hire me. I'd never *not* been able to get a job immediately. I was well-spoken in interviews and had a good employment history with sparkling references, but it seemed as though I had contracted some unemployability plague.

I Am All of Those People

My good friend at the time ran a candy store in the Mall of America, so out of pity she let me work there while I was searching. We would put our kids in the back room with activities and books—seated right within reach of carts full of every candy imaginable—while we served the customers out front. I'm sure my son, who was around five years old at the time, never wanted me to quit that job, but I couldn't stand it, and I didn't make enough to live on long term. But it sure was a blessing that helped me keep food on the table.

There was one restaurant, the Alamo Grill on the third floor of the mall, that I didn't at all want to work at, so I skipped it every time I went out to apply. But after a while, desperation took over. I was raising a son (and, by this time, a baby daughter) without help, and I couldn't afford to be picky any longer, so I went to the Alamo Grill and applied for a job as a waitress. They hired me immediately, and mild internal celebration ensued. There are a lot of places you want to be on Christmas and the weeks leading up to it. The Mall of America, for some people, is one of those places—unless you have to park there for work.

As far as the money was concerned, working at the Alamo Grill was much like working at any other restaurant. It was feast or famine, depending on the month or season and how much you made in tips. One of the welcome benefits was physically feasting when somebody screwed up an order and the food was up for grabs. We got half-price meals or sometimes free food after work. So eating like a queen on a waitress's budget wasn't too bad.

In the restaurant industry, you meet and work with a lot of interesting people. They tend to comprise one big dysfunctional family you just can't help but love. Many of them are high or drunk during and/or after work. So many of them sleep together, rotating partners as though there's no one else on the planet to date but coworkers.

Surprisingly, the crew at Alamo rated pretty normally on a scale of one to crazy. A bunch of us were college students; others were working there as a second job, with a professional enough day job to keep them operating above the "crazy" bar. I made some pretty good friends, some of whom I still occasionally connect with on social media some twenty-five years later. Or did until a few days ago when I yeeted off a cliff.

One of the people I met at the Alamo Grill ended up forever changing the course of my life. I'll call him Joe because that was really his name. I always describe Joe as Italian because he had a head of thick black hair. It might be racist to think everyone with thick black hair is Italian. I won't blow his cover here, but his last name started and ended with a K, so now I'm thinking he was probably Greek. His family was from the Midwest, and I'm not sure how many Italians would have migrated that way.

Joe had a permanent smile on his face unless he was

in the weeds. (Anyone who has worked in the restaurant industry probably has chills right now flashing back to their days in the weeds. For those who haven't had the pleasure, being "in the weeds" means you're buried so deep in food, customers, and orders, you can't see straight.)

One day he told me he had just moved to the area from Rapid City, South Dakota. I said, "Get out. I was born in Rapid City." He laughed and said, "Wow, wouldn't it be funny if one of my family members delivered you? All my uncles and the majority of my family are OB-GYN doctors in Rapid City."

It's hard to explain the wave of shock that went through my body as I told Joe, "That wouldn't be funny. That would be a miracle. I'm adopted, and I've been searching for my birth family for years."

I use the term "searching" very loosely. All along my parents told my brother and me we were adopted, so we never had a sit-down meeting that was some shock to our system. We just always knew. They adopted us both through adoption agencies. My brother lived in foster care a little longer than I did. I was adopted at six weeks old, and he at six months. My mom couldn't have children as a result of her severe diabetes, and after the stillbirth of one baby earlier in her life, the doctors told her she could die if she were to attempt another childbirth.

The search for my birth family began when I was probably thirteen years old. The curiosity was less "Who am I?" or "Where did I come from?" and more "How can I get out of here and meet the mystery people who will make me feel important?" That question finally got me to the point where I genuinely wanted to know more.

My mother had told me my adoption was arranged through an organization called Lutheran something or other. I asked her if she would help me find my birth family, and she took great offense to it. Being a mother myself, I can now understand why, but back then I couldn't.

It seemed like she was always trying to get rid of me (maybe because of my ridiculously spoiled bratty behavior that was absolutely intolerable on my best day), so why not help me fly the coop? I wanted to meet my birth family and get a slice of the dreamt-up trust fund that surely awaited me. I secretly hoped my natural mother was Madonna or someone equally cool—and, well, yeah, rich.

Sensing this to be the perfect opportunity, I commenced my solo teenage freedom quest. I called the adoption agency in South Dakota and asked them how to find my birth mother. They told me for $300 they would send a letter to her last known address to inquire whether or not she was interested in getting in contact with me. Well, it being 1983 and I being thirteen years old, $300 might as well have been $3 million.

I also wondered, *What are the odds she would even be at her last known location?* I figured somebody who gave up a child for adoption probably lived a transient, unstable, messed-up life, so that seemed too remote an option for me to pursue. That was the extent of my "search," and the dream just sort of died...until this conversation with Joe at the Alamo Grill ten years later.

I thought, *I can't pass up this opportunity to potentially meet my birth family through Joe's connections.* He asked me the name of the doctor who delivered me, and I said, "I have no idea."

When you're adopted, all the information you could use to track down your birth parents—names etc.—is redacted from your birth certificate and replaced with the names of your new adoptive parents, who can also change the name you were given at birth, as mine did.

I told Joe, "Maybe the doctor's name is still on the birth certificate." I went home that night extremely excited, looked it up, and found the name of the doctor who delivered me: Dr. Trappson. The next day at work, as soon as I saw Joe, I said, "Dang it! I forgot my birth certificate at home."

In an attempt to jog my memory, Joe began to recite a list of names of doctors who were in his family or with whom his family was associated. None of them sounded familiar until he said, "Dr. Trappson." My eyes widened to probably three times their normal size. I pointed at Joe and said, "Yes, that's it!" He laughed and said, "Dr. Trappson was my uncle's partner for years." The man standing before me in this ratty steakhouse actually knew the doctor who had delivered me.

I couldn't believe what was so effortlessly unfolding before me. Joe contacted his family and got me the doctor's home telephone number. I called and spoke to his lovely wife. She was so excited and said, "We would love to do anything we can to help you."

I spoke to the doctor later that same day. He, of course, was limited by privacy laws and rules and such about the information he could give me, but he was very helpful in guiding me on how to chase down medical records, determine whether I had siblings, and obtain other information.

Italian/Greek Joe also reached out to an attorney friend of his in Rapid City, who, for a mere $5, obtained a court order to open up my birth records and sent me a copy of my birth certificate—which had my birth mother's name, though no father was listed—along with a Rapid City phone book in case she or some family member with the same last name still lived in the area.

When that yellow envelope arrived in the mail, I stared at it way too long, and even after I had read every letter on the birth certificate, I still stared at it, knowing its importance but not its full value to me at the time. I opened the Rapid City phone book to the page listing the entries for the surname "Engelson" ("Mavis Engelson" was the mother's name listed on my birth certificate). For the record, speaking of names, my adoptive parents did me a huge solid by changing my name to Molly. My birth name was Marlys. M-A-R-L-Y-S. Gross!

I started with the first Engelson and called my way down the list. I didn't really put a lot of thought into what I was going to say, and I didn't write up a script beforehand. As they answered, I just asked them, "Do you happen to know a Mavis Engelson?" The first two or three said no, they didn't.

I got to the third or fourth number on the list and asked, "Do you happen to know Mavis Engelson?" The woman on the other end of the line replied, "Yes, I do. That's my daughter." If that moment were in a movie, you'd hear the sound effect of a needle scratching on a record, and the camera would quickly zoom in to show a close-up of my shocked facial expression. Time stood still. I was speaking to my maternal blood grandmother. That was when I realized a little preparation would've come in handy.

Oh my gosh! My thoughts were coming fast and furious, *Do I tell her who I am? What if her daughter never told her she had a child? What if I'm ruining this woman's life? What if I send her into a panic attack?* A whole lot of those "what ifs" could have been alleviated by a little bit of planning. I simply asked her with all the calm I could muster, "Do you know how I can get a hold of her?"

She replied, "Well, she's at work right now down at the grocery store. She should be home about ten o'clock this evening." I said, "Well, could you have her give me a call?" She said, "Sure. And may I ask, are you a friend of hers?" Again, time froze. *What do I say? Why didn't you plan ahead?* Preparation! Younger me had never been one to practice the precept that "preparation is key."

I couldn't lie, but neither could I tell the full truth. At some point, I imagined my birth mother looked at me or spoke to me or held me in her arms. So I simply said, "We knew each other a long time ago."

The woman on the phone said, "Okay, I'll have her call you when she gets home." Immediately after she hung up, I started second-guessing my words, as you do with any conversation or argument you ever engage in. I could have said this. I should have said that. I should have said something else. I shouldn't have called.

I thought, *This woman is going to call me, having no clue what is about to hit her. I'm going to have to break it to her, "Hey, I'm your child." Talk about an anxiety attack. Maybe I should have her mother break it to her first.*

My end game wasn't some lifelong mother/daughter

relationship. My main goal was just to let her know, "I'm okay." I was more mature now and didn't need to escape from the wonderful suburban life of my youth that, at the time, I thought was so awful and constricting. I just needed her to know I had a great life with great parents.

I basically grew up in Beaver Cleaver land. My parents gave me everything I could want and more. I was safe. I imagined my birth mother waking up on my birthday every year wondering if I was even alive. I wanted to thank her for not killing me. She could easily have had an abortion. I owed her that thanks because what she did wasn't easy. She was a hero. She was my hero.

I figured I should let somebody else be the bearer of random (not bad, just random) tidings. I called my birth grandmother back. "Hey, it's me again. I need to tell you who I really am." She listened as I explained what were—and what were not—my reasons for calling. "I don't want to interject myself into her life. I just want her to know I'm okay."

My birth grandma began to cry and said, "We have been searching for you our whole lives." I wondered if her definition of "searching" was as lame as mine. Maybe she just wanted to hide curiosities etc., but I took it for what it was. She said, "I will have her call you when she gets home," and we hung up.

I don't remember how long those hours between the

phone calls seemed, but I had twenty conversations in my head before the actual one transpired. The phone rang. Back in those days, we didn't have caller ID or cell phones, so it was just the ring of a landline, and you stared at it until you wanted to pick it up. I answered the phone. I said "hello" in a shaky, timid, trying-to-hold-it-together voice and heard the same inflection on the other end of the line.

I won't pretend to remember verbatim what she said, but she started by asking, "Hello, is this you?" She began to cry almost immediately. I said, "Yes, it's me." I do remember her saying, "You're still my daughter." I couldn't bear to hurt the woman's feelings, and I waged an internal argument, *This is all my doing. I'm turning her life upside down. No, I'm not your daughter. I have two wonderful parents who raised me, and I'm their daughter.* But I held those words in.

I told her all the things I wanted to tell her. I thanked her for not taking the easy road and killing me in utero and for allowing me to have the amazing life I had, for which she was really, in part, responsible. I wasn't angry or upset at all that she gave me up for adoption. I just wanted her to know I was okay and that she didn't have to tell anyone.

The mystery had been solved. She wasn't Madonna. There was no trust fund. She was still living with her mother and probably, at this point, was somewhere in her forties. I don't believe she went to college, and she spoke of multiple romantic relationships after the one that resulted in me. It sounded as though she had kind of a rough life.

She proceeded to tell me I did have siblings: two older brothers and two younger sisters. One brother had long black hair and looked like Steven Segal. He worked in nuclear science in the army. The other one, I remember, was successful, but I don't recall exactly what he did for a living. One of my sisters, I recall, earned a master's degree in communication, and the younger sister went to college as well. I was still struggling to finish my degree as a single mom.

Apparently, the Steven Segal lookalike was my only full sibling with whom I shared a father. I didn't even think when I was calling down the list in the phone book that I would find out the story of my birth, how my parents got together, or if they were ever together beyond the moments it took to make a baby. I didn't even think about asking those questions, but my birth mom told me anyway. She said she was with my father, broke up with him, and he subsequently came back and forced himself on her. So there it was: I was a product of rape, brought into the world in an act of trauma. It's ironic that I now have—had—a doctorate studying traumatology.

My birth mother told me a little more detail, and I wonder whether that story was just something she told her family to cover up for her mistake of going back to a guy they hated or to obscure some other bad decision. It's so easy to tell a small lie to your family just to save everyone from having to hear the truth, but I took her version for what it was. I never got my father's name and didn't ask who or where he was or whether he might have a trust fund for me. But I guess those questions never really go away.

I don't recall exactly how that initial phone call ended. I was glad to know a little bit about the family. One thing I do remember was her saying I was of Lakota descent, though I had no idea what that was. I think she probably used the term Sioux Indian and said something about moving off the reservation a couple of generations before my birth. I had no idea reservations still actually existed or that people still lived on them. All I knew, from the only history I was taught growing up in my all-White school, was that "reservation" was a word for an area of land that used to belong to a group of people I called the Indians. Oh, how my understanding has changed.

I gave my birth mom my address, and shortly after the phone call, she mailed me some pictures. The pictures of her were a bit out of focus, making it hard to tell the resemblance or even if there was one. She also sent me pictures of my grandparents on her side of the family and, I believe, a picture of one of my siblings, but that was it. I didn't call her again; the novelty had worn off. I knew what was and wasn't out there for me and had found out what

I needed to know. I was pacified. I was lacking nothing in family life, so there was no rush reunion meeting and certainly no field of daisies or streams of tears. It just was what it was.

Our conversation was over. I had let her know the things I felt she needed to know, but I wondered what the next few conversations in their house were like.

****

CHAPTER 3

Folks are still being ushered into the student center fellowship room, and I'm looking at a young man I don't recognize. He's maybe in his twenties and is sitting alone in the back of the room in a chair away from any of the full tables—arms folded like he's not too thrilled to be here. *I feel you, stranger. There are plenty of places I'd rather be too.*

His physical features are obviously Indigenous, so maybe he was dragged here by a family member on that side. Whoever he's with, he's clearly separating himself from the crowd on purpose, but little does he know he's actually painted a target on himself for one of my "people-loving" friends to come over and—*oh, here we go.*

"Hi! I'm Terry." My brother holds out his hand for a little longer than normal until the young man reluctantly shakes it and returns the greeting, "Joey." One word. This should be fun to watch because Terry is a talker. I'll hang here for a bit. Who says you can't enjoy your own funeral?

Then it hits me. Joey! Ah, yes! He and I were connected on social media. He was sitting with my Uncle Billy at the service. As I remember, we met during an open house at another university.

Terry balances his plate of spaghetti in one hand while he pushes a chair next to Joey with the other. "Where you from, Joey?"

"South Dakota."

The next obligatory funeral question, "How did you know Molly?"

"I didn't, really. I mean, we were friends on social media after we met on my campus once, but that's it. I'm here with Mr. Mills. I was visiting some family in Raleigh, so Mr. Mills and I decided to meet up while I was in the area. He had to do this first, though, so I tagged along." He catches himself calling my funeral a "had to do." *I get it, my friend.*

"I mean…" he stammers.

"It's okay; I haven't met a person yet who likes to go to these things." Terry was always so good at normalizing people's feelings and missteps to make them feel comfortable. I watched him do it on a daily basis, both growing up as kids and as adults in the office. We both worked together at Maxwell University, where I had gotten my undergraduate degree. He loves the Lord with his whole heart now and has a love for people to closely match. I'm not sure where Joey is with the Lord, but I do know this: He won't be the same after sitting with Terry. I can guarantee you that.

Joey half smiles. He returns the favor and asks, "Were you guys family?"

A pause. "She's my…"—Terry catches himself—"… was my sister." I'm glad to see I'm not the only one struggling with my was-ness. "And we worked together every day at the university we have here on the church campus."

There is a noticeable shift in Joey's demeanor when Terry says "church." Arms are folded again, and his half-smile turns to full frown. I know why. I think Terry does too. After all, he and I had many conversations about the reservation. The good, the bad, the ugly, the beautiful as I saw it. The statistics. The people who Terry knew by name. I'd report back after a service trip to the reservation, and he'd be the first to ask for an update. Many of our staff prayer meetings were peppered with his sincere prayers for my people there and for God to intervene on behalf of not only them but everyone on the reservation who was suffering in a multitude of ways.

His heart broke when I told him of the statistics, the individual stories of pain. I could see the care and concern in his eyes, but even more telling was that once he learned the truth of the reservation context (as best I could present it), he put his money where his mouth was or, more accurately, where his heart was. He always gave financially, and he donated his time and effort to mentor one on one a few young men on the reservation in an effort to instill hope.

Terry knows the reservation population is considered an unreached people group (UPG). This means there are not enough Indigenous evangelical Christians there to effectively share the gospel with their own nation. The implications of this are incredibly far-reaching. Even a brief glimpse into American history (the *reeeal* American history, not the quarter-truths and whole lies I learned in school) will explain the tension in the relationship between Christians and Indigenous populations.

"Not much of a church guy?" Terry asks in the first half of taking a bite of spaghetti. Brilliant. You can't take a question too seriously when it's being asked through a mouth full of food. That is Terry's intention. I know his modus operandi: keep it light and connect. "I get that. I wasn't either for a very long time."

He's so good at this. Better than I ever was. I hate that he could never quite clear his schedule enough to make it on one of the service trips to the reservation. He always wanted to go.

I could never bring myself to call it "the Rez." My Indigenous family there did, so it's not an offensive term among them, but it might be if an outsider tried to use it. And I always felt like an outsider, like I wasn't Indian enough. Heck, I wasn't Indian enough or White enough or enough in general...but I figure, "What are they going to do if I use the word Rez now—kill me?"

Joey's response to Terry's church question (if there was even going to be a response) is interrupted by the sound of a chair being dragged across the floor. Both men jump up to help my Aunt Little Dance, who is trying to balance her plate...with her drink...with her chair...with a tote bag stuffed to the gills. Two true gentlemen, clearly raised right, sprang into chivalrous action, one grabbing her plate and the other her chair. I still love to see men jump to help a damsel in distress, even though she is anything but.

She has a decades-long history of serving the reservation youth and working with programs helping the people with food security and education. She was listed as one of the "6 to Watch in 2016" in a Rapid City newspaper. She is probably best known for her work in suicide prevention, which is how we connected. Hers was one of the names Uncle Billy had given me during that first meeting at his house. When I mentioned my desire to serve in the areas of education and suicide intervention, he said I needed to talk to her.

He also told me she was my Aunt. Not like the aunts

in a European family tree. Those are pretty clearly your parents' sisters. I found out I have many aunts and uncles in the Lakota way of defining family. (Yes, "have." Here I can use present tense because those relationships will never die). My Uncle Billy, as a male elder in my family bloodline, gave me the option to call him Uncle or Grandfather. I chose Uncle, telling him he was far too young to be my Grandfather. He would always say that he didn't consider himself a tribal elder because that was a status based on how you had lived your life, and he was still working on it. At different events he'd refer to me sometimes as granddaughter and sometimes as his niece, maybe forgetting which I had originally chosen, but I didn't care, nor did I have any desire to correct him. I was just so grateful to be with blood family, they could have called me almost anything.

****

CHAPTER 4

During my first trip to the reservation, I had only seen Billy Mills Hall (the building named after my Uncle) briefly from the outside while passing by on our bus tour. It looked like a decent red brick building. But I would eventually get a different view. I was about to meet my Aunt Little Dance, who operated a youth center in the basement of that building. She shared space with a couple of administrative offices and the post office upstairs.

My daughter Mia and I were waiting outside in our rental car. My Aunt called and said she was waiting there too. I didn't see her, and I panicked, thinking I was at the wrong building. I was never late to a meeting, and the thought of being late to our first meeting caused me to panic. I hope I was on time for my funeral. Sorry—corny dead girl joke.

As it turned out, we were merely on opposite sides of the building. I pulled the car around to her side of the building, passing a group of men sitting by the dumpster. I drove by that side of the building many times during my subsequent visits to the youth center and was invariably confronted with that same picture. Sometimes the players would change, but the story was the same. I often wept in sadness for the symbolism—and the reality—of that scene: young, able-bodied men who could be the strong pillars of their community, spending their days languishing by the commercial trash bin, companioned by a number of stray scavenging dogs.

It was as though they reckoned themselves as rubbish, counted their value as zero—or less—and threw themselves away with the trash. I made an inner vow to invest all my strength and resources and enlist others to change that self-destructive paradigm and try to give those precious men hope and courage.

I spotted my Aunt sitting in a red sedan. She was with her best friend Ellen, who was actually more like a sister connected by a deep love for their people, particularly the youth. They were bound together by a cause to stop the suicides of both adults and kids. They both have families who must be the most gracious on the planet, as those two women are constantly on the go, serving their community, hosting activities, and making middle-of-the-night suicide intervention crisis response runs.

A man named Sean attended our meeting too. He worked alongside my Aunt and Ellen, serving the youth

Dr. Diane Sharp

center, and I believe they said he was once a participant in the youth program.

We went inside, and they gave me a tour of the youth center. Two parallel stairwells, separated by a hallway, led into the basement. There were locked doors on either side of the bottom of the stairs. We went through one of the doors, down a hallway, and through another door locked by a loose padlock hanging on by two very loose screws that would provide no challenge whatsoever to a half-determined trespasser.

The door opened into a surprisingly well-lit brown-paneled room. To the left stood a white bookshelf filled with books, some newer, some very outdated, and some you could tell were mere rejects donated from someone's decades-old collection. The donors' intention was to do the right thing. I'm a book lover, too, and I know it is difficult to throw books away. I fully understand keeping them years past their prime. I wonder whether there will be books where I finally land.

The walls were adorned with artwork, drawings, and pictures done by the youth. There were some posters clearly penned by children with slogans of encouragement concerning education, Lakota pride, or suicide prevention. I could feel the pride of the artists as they drew and colored these masterpieces. They all pointed to the theme that "life is worth living."

All the furniture was old, some beyond restorative cleaning, with most pieces past their structural integrity's prime. But they were making it work, providing a safe place for the youth to find some hope.

A door at the rear of the room led into an area with concrete cinder-block walls reminiscent of an unfinished basement or underground garage. It was filled a third of the way to the ceiling with a mountain of unsorted donations: boxes and piles of clothes, diapers, blankets, toiletries, and food. Along the wall behind the door stood a couple of refrigerators and a reach-in deep freezer. Maybe they worked, and maybe they didn't because they also doubled as shelves with nonperishable food stacked on top, with more on the floor.

It was glaringly apparent the center's personnel were overwhelmed with sorting through donations, 80 percent of which was most likely unusable trash donated by the thoughtless. Though the rest could be repurposed into something valuable, very few of the items sported the sheen of newness.

The food—marginally nutritious fare, such as Vienna sausages and ramen noodles—was loosely organized on the shelves to allow someone to quickly pack and give a box to someone in need to temporarily fill their stomachs until their hunger pangs returned.

Furniture items, an enormous old floor model big

screen TV, an older PlayStation and other gaming consoles, and other items were randomly strewn wherever an empty spot was available. Time simply did not allow for organizing the goods immediately upon receipt. There was too much surviving to do. The center clearly needed teams of people to do the organizing, and I knew I could easily form a team of my people back home to come and perform that task.

The large gymnasium upstairs was used for basketball games, giveaways, food and clothing distributions, and other community activities. A small tribal flag next to the scoreboard was dwarfed by the vast white walls. Leaning against a wall in one corner was a mural of Uncle Billy's Olympic finish line victory painted on a piece of plywood.

A few bleacher-style seats were pressed against the walls. One side of the room looked like it was used more for storage than for activities. Aunt Little Dance explained, "This is the only place in town large enough to hold funerals, so when someone dies, we have to cancel our youth activities." Between the suicides and the mortality rates, funerals occurred far more often than they should.

The building was so dilapidated that when a funeral or any other large gathering took place upstairs, the pipes leaked raw sewage directly into the youth center in the basement whenever the restrooms were used. There were piles of cat litter on the floor. They told me that was to cover up the raw sewage. The tribal council's answer to the youth center's repair requests was to just give them cat litter!

Aunt Little Dance and Ellen knew of some people with the proper equipment who were willing to dig, find, and repair the leak. They only had to get permission from one individual in the tribal leadership, who, for one reason or another, refused to give it. Not only do the people on the reservation have to battle poverty and generations of oppression and trauma, but they have to fight misconduct in their own ranks and battle their own people. It takes a very special eye to see the potential to win against those odds, and these two ladies have those eyes. They smile; they laugh through all of it, and they talk expectantly about hope and change. They are definitely my people.

****

CHAPTER 5

Dr. Stone was my boss at the university, the best boss you could ever have. He taught me more about grace and leadership than all the leaders combined I had in the decades before him. He's standing in the back of the room, occasionally rocking on his feet, lifting up to his tiptoes, looking left and right, nose in the air. Not out of arrogance (not an ounce of that in him), but he's scanning the room, like I'd seen him do so many times before, looking to make sure everyone is being taken care of. He'd never dream of sitting down when others are standing.

Strange for a leader, right? Not with my people. They're servant leaders who genuinely serve, equip, and empower their people. That's how they won my heart. I always said I could work with just about anyone, but I won't work *for* just anyone. Working with leaders like Dr. Stone is what kept me at this university for more than twenty years. I sure loved it here.

I Am All of Those People

Since we're in the student center on the university campus, Dr. Stone is sort of the unofficial host of the day by default. I always thought I was a pretty smart person... until he walked in the room. He is a vault of knowledge of history, the Bible, theology, and law pertaining to Indigenous people, and he houses all of that with the greatest degree of genuine humility I've ever seen. He loves to teach. He is president of the university, but I think if he had his way, he'd just teach.

"Dr. Stone, why don't you come sit down and take a load off?" Terry beckons him over to where they are all sitting. Dr. Stone does another scan of the room. I can tell he desperately wants to get off his feet, but the innate need to serve others initially holds him back. I guess he establishes to his satisfaction that everyone is okay because he grabs the first available chair and brings it to the area, now forming an impromptu cluster. Two of the participants nudge their chairs apart, and Dr. Stone situates his chair in the space to complete the circle.

By this time Ellen had joined the group, sitting next to my Aunt. They had their own side conversation going on. They'd look at someone in the room, giggle, and eventually one of them would elbow the other to stop before they were caught laughing at folks. I can't blame them for two reasons. One, I was queen of the people watchers, and two, this room was definitely an eclectic island of misfit toys all dressed in black.

Again, the prefatory squeal of the microphone. Then, "Can I have your attention, please? We don't anticipate it taking much longer, and we will make an announcement when it is clear for you to reenter. Thank you so very much for your patience."

A muffled groan sweeps through the room like a really sorry version of the wave at a football stadium when only half the crowd participates. I guess everyone in the room is trying to be on their best behavior so they won't be seen as the unrefined side of the family. I have one of those sides, believe me. I wonder why none of them have showed up yet. Maybe they won't? Maybe...

While I was watching my Aunt and Ellen people-watch, Dr. Stone had given a short history of our friendship and was starting to walk them through the annals of our time working together at the university.

Terry's teenage son approaches with one of his friends. "Dad, can I have some money to run to the gas station to get some snacks?" Terry pulls out his wallet and hands him some cash. The teens take off for the door. I think some of the grownups wish it were them hitting the exit.

"Man, anyone else's kids do that to them? I'm going to be in the poorhouse before he graduates!" Everyone laughs with nods of understanding.

Ellen nods and chuckles, "Mine do it all the time! They can just smell when I have an extra dollar."

Aunt Little Dance nods in agreement and quips, "Mine will pick my pockets when I die. I'm sure of it."

She and Dr. Stone simultaneously pull the lining of their pants pockets out, and everyone laughs together. "Isn't that what parents are for?" asks Joey with a smile, encapsulating the universal understanding of child-induced broke-ness.

The air feels a little lighter. Laughter at a shared life experience does that. That's why sitcoms are so successful. We all have so many things in common, so many painful experiences at which the only thing one can do is laugh.

Dr. Stone addresses Aunt Little Dance, "I understand you run the youth center on the reservation. It is nice to finally meet you. Molly always loved bringing the teams there. I always knew she was about to go when her office started to look like a formalwear store bursting at the seams."

She laughs and slowly nods her head. "She brought so many beautiful dresses for our prom outreach."

I loved doing that. It was the first time I felt like I was actually making a difference there and had a place, somewhere that I fit.

If there's an activity or an event on the reservation, you can bet Aunt Little Dance and Ellen are there, and my Aunt usually has a microphone in her hand running the show. She helps organize, host, and DJ the proms. They operate their own form of "walk the red carpet," collecting formalwear from all over the country for the youth who don't have anything to wear to the prom.

Aunt Little Dance ventures in her soft voice, "We work in suicide prevention," nodding her head toward Ellen. "We started years ago as a youth literacy program, encouraging kids to read with the understanding that reading does so much for people and allows them access to a world much bigger than just their immediate surroundings.

"We teach them, 'Reading can educate you. It can expand your vocabulary and make you a more articulate speaker and writer. Reading can open you up to an entirely new world. You are never stuck anywhere as long as you have a book to transport your mind to another place and time.'"

Dr. Stone nods and leans in to hear her. All she had to say was "books," and he was captivated. He and I shared a love for reading and often spoke of our frustration that we had a library full of books at the university, but we could never read them all. Nerds, I know.

Ellen continues Aunt Little Dance's narrative, "The program eventually morphed into a suicide intervention program because the need was so great for something to curb the climbing suicide rates among the reservation's youth, which is five times the national average. There was a state of emergency declared on the reservation multiple times due to the high number of suicides. We knew something had to be done, so we refocused the program."

Anyone can talk about tragedy and complain, "Something needs to be done!" But I watched these two women back up their words with their money and their time. They have undoubtedly saved countless lives in the process.

Ellen continues, "The kids who go through the program—some have no parents and are being raised by a grandparent who is struggling to survive. Some come to us with no coat in the winter and holes in their shoes. We give them food, clothes, toiletries, whatever we have on our shelves in the youth center.

"We try to show them a love that causes them to leave better than they came. They're taught family values. They're taught the value of community. They're taught the value of loving themselves and other people. They're taught the value of service. Sometimes we travel as a group to different churches, schools, and youth groups, doing presentations on how valuable life is and that it is indeed worth living.

"We give speeches to let the world know we are here and will visit any organization that will host us so we can educate the world on what's really happening on the reservation and how that organization can partner to help.

Dr. Diane Sharp

I always say, 'Together we can do anything; we can bring about change.'"

Terry chimes in with, "Wow, that is amazing work! We have been praying for you here at the university for years, ever since Molly's first trip. My heart was broken when I learned what was really happening there. I had no idea or at least little idea. Her stories really broke my heart. My wife and I tried to give as much as we could to her trips. Thank you for the work you do."

"Thank *you*," says Aunt Little Dance. "Without your giving and caring, we couldn't do it." Ellen nods in agreement.

By this time the conversation has captured the attention of a nearby table of onlookers. A handful of them scoots their chairs into a concentric arc behind the circle occupied by Dr. Stone, Aunt Little Dance, and the others.

I recognize the group as some of my high school classmates. They came to pay their respects and, no doubt, hold a mini-reunion of their own.

I see Mark and Deanna, the quintessential embodiment of the proverbial "high school sweethearts get married" story. Mark, the jock who lettered in football, track, and baseball, looks like he's kept himself in pretty good shape. Deanna is just as beautiful as the day she was crowned prom queen her senior year.

Patrick, the perennial troublemaker in school, takes his seat, and I can tell by his expression that he intends to push some envelopes. Classic Patrick. This should be entertaining—and, I suspect, not a little annoying.

The two others I hardly remember. They were both pretty quiet and kept to themselves, but I always got along with them. I think the guy is named Jeremy, and she is—I wrack my brain for the name—Sheila or Shelly or something like that. Yes, it's Sheila. I don't expect either of them to say much, but I might be surprised.

We all took the same American history class and were all fed the same defective and deceptive lessons about the issues at hand here. It will be interesting to see whether and how any of my classmates may have, through their life experiences and perhaps independent study, recovered from the indoctrination.

"Why are they so poor on the reservation?" interrupts Patrick. "What's the problem?" *Well, that didn't take long.*

All the Indigenous people in the group smile a knowing smile, indicating they had heard this question a million times before. I heard my Uncle talking to another Indigenous friend one time about his visit to a group of White people, and they joked:

"Did they ask you *the* question?"

"You mean, 'What's *the* problem?'?"

Dr. Diane Sharp

Everyone, including me, looks at Aunt Little Dance after Patrick's question, silently waiting for the answer. I know it's a silly/ignorant question (in the nicest meaning of the word, because when I was introduced to the plight of reservation life, I asked that one myself), but I wanted to hear how she answered it. So many people asked me this question on more than one occasion, and I usually fumbled with an answer the best I could.

Auntie explains, "There is a myriad of issues. If it were a singular problem, it would have been fixed by now. We are smart people. If we weren't, we would be extinct."

"Like the colonists wanted," Jeremy mumbles to himself, though a little louder than he probably wanted to. *Well, whaddaya know? Maybe high school lies aren't forever after all.*

Auntie eases Jeremy's embarrassment with a welcoming smile, a nod, and a twinkle in her eyes. "But we are still here," she continues. "We are strong and resilient." Adopting a more serious tone, she says, "But the generational trauma brought on from the beginning of colonization has lasting scars that are still impacting our people. There's just so much pain." She speaks with a gentle intensity and authority that organically makes everyone else listen intently.

"We have to let people know what reservation life is really like for the young people. For all of us."

"You really believe they don't know?" Joey sneers. "They know; they just don't care." He turns his head away from the group, looking for Uncle Billy to come and rescue him from the rigorous conversation. I think he realized he just got lippy with an elder. Reengaging with the group, he leans in like he just had to get it off his chest and, this time, addresses the White people in the circle rather than Auntie.

"You come with your church groups every summer in your white vans full of do-gooders. All you want is to check a box in your own soul that you did something to make yourself feel good or to post on social media for other people to think you're doing something good. You just want to assuage your White guilt. We don't need your help."

None of the White people who hears his challenge responds, and, true to form, Patrick straightens up in his chair and piggybacks on Joey's comments with a theatrical vicarious diatribe, exaggerating his words for full effect. Oh, I forgot to mention Patrick was a natural in our high school drama club.

"White guilt? What the heck is White guilt? I've never heard of that. I sure don't have any White guilt. Guilt for what? For what happened 500 years ago? How am I responsible for what some pilgrim did? And frankly, you needed us! This place wasn't civilized until the pilgrims came. Columbus came a long time ago. If that ancient history still bothers you, then you need therapy. How would you even have gotten the Bible if it weren't for Christian missionaries? All I'm saying is I've never done anything to you. Don't blame me for what someone else did."

"Ancient history? You mean my grandma?" Joey retorts with thinly veiled contempt. "She was in one of the boarding schools where they cut her hair and beat her if she spoke her language. She told us the stories at the dinner table. Does that sound like ancient history to you?"

Ellen exhales and says with a smile, "Young man, we have to build bridges." She wasn't disagreeing with what Joey said, just the way he was going about it. "These people are nice. They come up every summer to help with our kids' camps and summer programs. We get very little help from the tribe or our own people or even the teens on the reservation during summer camp. They wouldn't run without the church groups that come."

"We have to work together if we want to see change," Auntie adds.

"The White way isn't always the right way," Joey retorts. "The reservation needs to be changed *by* the people on the reservation. We can take care of it ourselves."

Auntie nods as Ellen replies, "Yes, that would be nice, but where are they? When money does come in, the council is so corrupt that nothing can get done. They talk about how important it is for kids to get an education or learn a skill, but then they'll only hire or award grants to their family members and friends. We need to focus on the corruption in our own tribal system before we can point fingers at people who are at least trying to help."

Remembering why they were here in the first place, Auntie brings up our last trip to the reservation. "Molly and her teams worked so hard when they came up. I saw their tears. They were real. They prayed for us, and they meant it."

Joey smirks. "Why couldn't they have been the ones on the Nina or the Pinta?"

Auntie continues, "They wanted to work so hard to do all of the projects we needed to have done, but the truth is our own people should be doing the work. Our teens should be cleaning up their families' and neighbors' yards. We shouldn't need outside people to come and do it for us. It's embarrassing that we have so many people who are so high and drunk that we can't even take care of our homes, our parks…the kids would have nowhere clean to play if it weren't for the groups coming up in the summer. I try to tell our youth to have pride in their home. The reservation can be a beautiful place."

Ellen recounts a story, "We needed some things moved around one day while Molly and the team were there, remember that?" She looks at Auntie, who smiles and nods. "She wanted to pay local helpers to do work."

"Excuse me," ventures Mark. "Shouldn't all outside groups do that? It doesn't seem right that they come up and do all these construction projects, taking work away from the people on the reservation who need those jobs to feed their families."

Ellen continues, "I took Molly to pick up the trustees." Auntie and Joey share a knowing smile.

Oooh, yes, I remember that day. I thought I was kind of a big deal getting to meet with some of the tribal trustees. Alas, my pride. Ugh.

"I didn't tell her who the trustees were. We went to the prison and got up to the window…"

I thought we were just going to make a stop for Ellen to visit someone. They were *always* making unscheduled stops to see someone or to deliver something someone needed. I got so used to those detours I didn't even ask why we were there.

"I told the deputy we were there to sign out and pick up some trustees. Molly's eyes got as big as the moon, and she said, 'I'm sorry?'"

Okay, in my defense, how could I know the trustees were inmates considered trustworthy enough to be checked out of prison to work?

Ellen goes on to explain to the group who they were and does an exaggerated impersonation of my reaction with her eyes big and eyebrows raised. Her voice cracks like mine did, and everyone roars with laughter. Well, I always said I wanted laughter at my funeral, and I'm cool with it, even if it's at my expense.

Those trustees had the best attitudes and were so respectful to Ellen and kind to everyone. We had such a blast. I'm going to miss those trips. I hope we did some good. I hope we made a difference.

Auntie adds, "I always made her ask me before she bought any jewelry or anything from the local people who tried to sell things to her group. Whenever some people hear that a church group has arrived, they get dollar signs in their eyes, but I never want to enable their alcohol or drug problems by giving them money, so we have to be smart about who we buy things from."

As the conversation is lightening, Ellen sits back and softly remarks, "I hope your teams will still come now that she's gone."

Terry quickly responds, "My family and I would love to come and work with you. Thank you for welcoming us. We weren't sure if we could still come now that Molly is gone or even if we'd even be welcome there."

Auntie raises a finger like a grandmother teaching a very important lesson (because that's exactly what she is doing). She speaks slowly and succinctly with intention. "We honor her bloodline. She is family. I told her she could bring any team she wanted to do whatever work she wanted—with us and for us. I extend to you the same invitation because you are her people. You are the people of my niece."

Silence follows as everyone drinks in the gravity of her authority as an elder from the reservation and understands in that moment the power that comes with that role.

"Thank you," Terry says through the tears welling up in his eyes. "We really just want to help the right way to address the need."

"That's the problem." Joey's words are laced with frustration. "Who in your scenario determines the need? You? What makes you think you know what we need, much less have anything to offer us that we don't already have?

"Let me give you an example. We had a group come up and buy a car for a family who lived in a remote area of the reservation, just far enough from the center of town to seem inconvenient to outsiders but easily walkable. The family members would walk together to the store to get their groceries or rely on their friends and family to take them shopping. It worked fine for them, but the church group couldn't imagine living without a car, so they just went out and bought one.

"Come to find out, the reason they didn't have a car was that the father was an alcoholic, and he had crashed the last three cars they had. The mother never wanted to have another car around for him to drive, so she would walk to the store with her kids. She loved this time with them to tell them stories of their ancestors, and she used the time alone with them to solve any family problems they might be having. Sometimes she and her husband would walk together to get some exercise and bond as a married couple.

"Well, after the church group bought them this car, they lost the valuable time they spent together walking, as they now had access to a ride everywhere. The church group wanted them to be able to get their children to activities where they could build some resilience and connect with people in a way the White people saw fit.

"But they already had that! They were already connected to their parents and their siblings—our way. These connections build resilience in our youth to stay out of trouble and away from drugs and alcohol. Well, that family ended up more distant from each other, and the kids got into a wide array of trouble. I haven't seen any of them in a long time."

Ellen says, "Their father died. Drunk driving last summer."

"So what is it you think you have of any value to help

us?" Joey asks this calmly but as a definite challenge and with an intensity that makes the air feel heavy. He is looking directly at Terry, so no one else dares to answer. They, too, look at Terry.

After a bit of a pause, Terry humbly offers, "Molly always spoke of hope and the need for hope on the reservation. She told us all about youth who tried to kill themselves because they felt they had nothing to hope for. I guess all I have to offer is hope as I know it." I can feel the sincerity in his voice. I hope my people can too. "I only have my experience, which tells me that my hope only comes from—"

"If you say Jesus...!" Joey verbally lashes at him so loudly, others around the room look over toward the circle of chairs to see the commotion.

Auntie and Ellen emit simultaneous "Shhhhhhs." Joey quiets down but continues, "We heard that name before. We heard the White man say, 'We are here to help you,' and they gave us blankets laced with smallpox and kidnapped Native children and took them to their boarding 'schools,' never to be seen again. The lucky ones were beaten and returned to their families. The others? Read the news. Those are the bodies they're finding under the old boarding schools now. Hundreds and hundreds of bodies of small children, *my* ancestors," he says, pounding his chest. "Those were no schools!" he utters with clear disdain.

"The nuns and priests abused those children in every way imaginable 'with a rod in one hand and a Bible in the other,' as Grandma used to say. Some of her friends and cousins who were taken with her never came back home. Mothers wailed for their children who were taken away by the Christians to kill the Indian in them. So your Jesus? No, thank you!"

He pauses, takes a breath, and speaks a little more slowly and less excitedly, "Well, they're coming home now. We're digging them up and bringing our children home—as bones."

Dark silence descends over the group as everyone takes in what he is saying. I see tears in Terry's eyes as he listens with his ears and his heart, as he always did when I spoke of the pain I saw and heard on my trips to the reservation. Sheila and Deanna are also touched by the words as they both reach into their purses for a tissue to dab their eyes.

After what seems like an eternity, Sheila clears her throat and meekly asks, "Did that really happen the way he says? Did the church really do that?" For some reason she directs her questions to Dr. Stone, not in a challenging way but with a voice registering shock, but with the hope she'll hear something to make sense of what was just heard.

Ever the peacemaker, Dr. Stone speaks up in his usual gentle way that carries authority more because of the accuracy of his words than any force in his voice. "I'm sorry." He directs his apology at Joey, Auntie, and Ellen, looking each of them in the eyes after he repeats the phrase. How long have they waited to hear these words from someone who took responsibility for the painful acts clearly committed initially by others but prolonged by people like me who just didn't know?

"The truth of the matter," Dr. Stone continues, "is we are all responsible for repairing the damage done, not only by people claiming to operate as the church but by a dominant culture of which we are a part. We must acknowledge that as fact if we want to do any good going forward. We can keep our heads in the sand and live our lives safely apart from others—or we can seek out the truth of history and strive to do better."

My first thought races to: *I never learned any of this in school.*

"I never learned any of this in school," Terry mirrored my thought, "until Molly told us a little about it, and I researched and found out it was true…and worse."

Ellen looks at Terry. "I like to hear you talk about researching for the truth. You're not going to get the truth in schools; that's for sure. I remember in elementary school being taught a song about Columbus and his ships. I can still hear it in my head, 'The Nina, the Pinta, the Santa Maria…'" She and Auntie giggle. "There were so few Indian teachers when I went to school. We learned the White version of history at the government-run schools on the reservation. We knew it wasn't right because of what our families told us, but we had to learn it because that was the only school for us."

"That problem still exists," Joey says. "We need more Native teachers. How can White people tell our children anything about history or their life experience on the reservation? You know what they say, 'The one who wins the war writes the history.' That's why it's so flawed."

"You see, we learned in school that Columbus was some big war hero. That's why he's got Columbus Day," says Terry.

"Indigenous People's Day," all three Indigenous people in the circle say at once. Everyone laughs.

"Jinx!" says Ellen. "You owe me a soda."

"Speaking of soda, I'm going to get me something to drink. Can I get y'all anything?" asks Terry.

"I'll take one," Auntie raises her hand. I raise mine too, but nobody notices. Hey, it was worth a shot.

"I'm good," says Joey.

"While you do that, Terry, I'm going to see if I can get some sort of update." Dr. Stone walks over to a member of the church staff and returns to the circle with an update.

Dr. Diane Sharp

"There's nothing to report. The situation is exactly as it was before." I notice I don't mind waiting like I used to. I, as an alive person, was so impatient. Now, where else do I have to be? I imagine God will take me up out of here when He chooses, so I am enjoying my last few minutes in close proximity to my people.

Terry returns with an armload of sodas and water and loads everyone up with a couple of bottles of each, whether they asked for it or not. He was always so generous, even if it wasn't well thought out. That's how he loved people. And something tells me that's his way of saying sorry today. To my people.

While passing the drinks out, he says, "I'm interested to know more about the war history."

"I'll share with you what I shared with Molly when she sent me the manuscript for her book," replies Dr. Stone. "Did you all know she was writing a book?"

Some nod, and some react in surprise. The fact is I never got to finish it. I thought it would make some sort of difference, so I sent it to Dr. Stone for him to look over and tell me his thoughts. And boy, did he! It was garbage, and I knew it. He knew it, too, and gently broke it to me wrapped in a nice bow of constructive criticism. It stunk, plain and simple. The *only* reason I was writing it was that I had to find a way to build bridges between all my circles: my Christian, my White, and my Indigenous people.

I Am All of Those People

All eyes watch him as he steps over to a table by the entrance door and picks up a stack of papers. As he returns to his seat, I am stunned to see he is carrying my final manuscript.

"I brought Molly's manuscript today so I could read a few excerpts that represent her heart when it came my turn to speak. When we were evacuated from the room, something"—he looks skyward and grins—"or someone told me to bring this here.

"I think you'll all find it revelatory. She was on the right track, and it had promise to be very good."

Did he just lie in church? The first (frankly, the first three) draft(s) were complete drivel. But perhaps he was (over)selling my work to take full advantage of this captive audience.

CHAPTER 6

And so the class began. "There were some areas concerning history where she just didn't initially have enough information to complete the picture, but we were well on our way to shore that up. My own wife is an enrolled tribal member. I have learned so much from her quiet yet powerful wisdom that guides a family in the way only a woman can. It's quite difficult to talk about 'Native American' history or beliefs or traditions because there are so many different tribes, and each of them have a very unique experience. Even posing a question about 'Indigenous people and how they reconcile God and Christianity' makes an erroneous assumption. American Indians aren't a monolithic group who all practice the same religion or even hold to the same cultural traditions. There is *no* singular way American Indian people in all the tribes—from the Lakota in the plains region to the Crow in Montana, the Cahuilla to the Seminole—all have unique languages and beliefs. And *many* are Christian.

So often there is the erroneous assumption that their religious traditions and beliefs are so much different from Christianity. I think you'll all be surprised to know that humans tend to be more alike than they are different.

"It was clear Molly had a heart to tell the world about the impact of historical papal bulls and the Doctrine of Discovery. But that's only a small part of the big picture of colonization. Catholics weren't the only ones who came and laid claim to the land here. Over the years there were Pilgrims, Puritan Calvinists, Quakers, Jesuits, Church of England and Episcopalians, and so on."

As I listen to Dr. Stone speak, I relive my admiration for his mastery of the facts and his heartfelt passion for getting the truth out to as many as will listen.

"And the boarding schools…" I can see the still fresh pain on the faces of all my Indigenous people in the circle. "One present front-burner trauma for many Native Americans is the boarding school era, which began with the Carlisle School in Pennsylvania in 1879. It was a deep stain in American history. Native American children were kidnapped and taken to the 'schools'—actually, indoctrination centers—to be forcibly assimilated into the colonial culture and religion. To strip the children of their identities, school officials cut off their long, glorious hair and beat them if they were caught speaking their native language. The traumas these children suffered continued for generations, their blood carrying the tragic unresolved memories to their children and their children's children.

"Boarding schools were—and are—a leading cause of trauma among Native Americans. Through institutions like Carlisle, founded by Richard Henry Pratt, a cavalry captain, the American government forcibly removed Native children and placed them in schools to 'kill the Indian and save the man,' forcing assimilation by stripping them of their language, culture, and family ties. In addition to cutting their hair to shame and subjugate these small children, the physical and sexual abuse that occurred have left behind lasting effects that still present a challenge to healing. There was a 50 percent mortality rate at the schools."

"Children…children…my ancestors." Joey's voice fades. He snaps out of his drifting thoughts and boldly reengages, his face switching from a sad far-off gaze to attentive focus on the topic at hand.

Aunt Little Dance chimes in, "Molly and I had one relative in common who was in one of those schools. She is still alive and attended our last family reunion. Think about the implications of that. The surviving 'students' and their families are still dealing with the trauma and telling the stories of horrific abuse at the hands of those claiming to know and serve this Christ. Think about how this alone is a great barrier to now introducing the idea of a relationship with Christ to Indigenous people."

"Perhaps boarding school trauma doesn't seem very far back in history now?" Joey looks briefly toward my high school classmates. Stunned, uncomfortable silence hangs heavy in the air, even heavier than your average run-of-the-mill uncomfortable funeral air.

"It amazes me that it took this long for me to hear of this part of history," says Terry, shaking his head. "The schools I went to made the colonists out to be the heroes and the Indians to be savages. And just think, if I didn't learn the truth in school, odds are the people who are voted into office didn't either. And here they are making decisions that impact the nation, with no *real* understanding of the truths of history that still impact Indigenous people."

"Every. Single. Day," Joe adds softly.

"So, at the risk of sounding stupid, what *is* this Doctrine of Discovery you keep talking about?" Sheila asks sheepishly.

"And paper bulls?" follows Deanna.

"*Papal* bulls," Dr. Stone gently corrects her, "a fancy term for declarations made by the pope, and you're not stupid, Sheila. Very few know what these things are and, more importantly, what they set into motion in America. The Doctrine of Discovery is very complex.

"Basically it is this: The Catholic Church was the political power structure. The pope made a declaration in 1493, which simply said any new lands found could only belong to the first Christian monarch who discovered them. Then they claimed the lands they wanted as long as they weren't currently occupied by other Christians. After they took what they wanted, they could open it for any European person to lay claim to the land *they* wanted.

"Imagine the Doctrine of Discovery is the stone foundation of a structure. By itself it isn't a tall, strong building, but it is the foundation upon which much was built in our nation and the rest of the world for many years after.

"When the claiming of occupied land was exercised in what is now the United States, the Indigenous people already living here had to then come under the international rule of law. Those were the first stones on the foundation.

"In 1830 President Jackson encouraged westward expansion by settlers. Referring to the Indigenous population as 'wandering savages,' he made and broke treaties regularly to engage in land theft. The promised "humane removal" didn't happen. Cherokee men, women, and children loved by God were removed from their homes and forced to close to 1,000 miles in the harsh winter, where 4,000 of 16,000 Cherokee died along what we now call the Trail of Tears.

"In the late 1800s, Manifest Destiny was originally coined in a passing note in a newspaper article. But the concept found traction among the growing sentiment that taking the land from American Indians was the right of the settler. And another floor was added to the building.

"A number of court cases have cited the Doctrine of Discovery as the precedent to remove the land ownership rights of American Indians in the US, all of which justified the land theft. Stone upon stone, floor upon floor was being built.

"Eventually many Indigenous people gave up their ways in order to salvage some land and voting rights. They gave up their songs, their dances, and their traditions, creating a cultural vacuum for their descendants. Another floor.

"Can you see how much in America has been and continues to be built on this faulty foundation? We now have an enormous national structure in place of generational privilege for some and generational trauma for others. It must be dismantled stone by stone—and that's a big job."

As though five light bulbs just lit up above their heads, my classmates all nod in agreement. Not only do they realize they had been lied to in our American history classes, but they now learn the perpetuating ripple effects of ignorance and deception about the issues all the way up to statehouses and Capitol Hill.

"And it doesn't stop with historical westward expansion

decisions," says Joey, leaning back in and reengaging intellectually in the conversation. "They're still signing decisions into law based on faulty intel and flawed precedent. These laws will continue to govern our right to own property until they are changed. The Doctrine of Discovery should never have been endorsed, and yet here it is, referenced and validated in modern-day court decisions that impact our ability to keep and own our lands. The pope just this year finally acknowledged that the bulls leading to the doctrine have no legal or moral authority. Finally."

"That is true," Dr. Stone affirms, opening the manuscript to the relevant passages he will read, no doubt seamlessly blending my scribblings with his own incisive commentary.

"The validation of the Doctrine of Discovery is perhaps the most sweeping betrayal by the White man because it undergirds and justifies all other forms of abuse, and that justification was dispensed by those who were supposed to be guardians of personal and property rights and their resultant freedoms."

I envision Dr. Stone in a classroom or before a congressional committee as he adopts the teaching tone I have heard many times before. I wonder if the others within earshot know they are in for a lengthy and brilliant dissertation that will keep them on the edge of their seats.

"They didn't attack us hand to hand with swarms of military-attired soldiers wielding swords and guns," he reads. "No, we were stabbed in the back by a stroke of the pen held by a handful of black-robed justices who probably never came within a hundred miles of the land they ripped from under our feet and the millennia-old ways of life they slashed from our culture."

Dr. Stone continues, "The US Supreme Court was barely three decades old when, in 1823, it decided—unanimously, without a single hint of dissent—a land dispute case known as Johnson & Graham's Lessee v. McIntosh. The legal fight involved two parties claiming real estate, one who inherited the land their ancestors bought from Native Americans and the other who received a government land patent.

"In a decision that has never been overturned, bolstered by condescending invective against Indigenous people, the court ultimately ruled that the Native Americans had no right to sell their land, except to the federal government. In essence, the court converted the rights of Indigenous people in the land to a mere 'right of occupancy' terminable at will by the federal government.

"There was no legal justification for the ruling, only the abracadabra waving of the Discovery Doctrine wand to make their rights disappear. In fact, most of the dictum of the opinion discussed the doctrine, where the court carefully weighed the interests of the United States, the individual colonies and states therein, various foreign countries, agents, and entities—without one thought of consideration for those who were the unwilling party to those conquests, contracts, and treaties and who suffered the greatest victimization from the doctrine: Native Americans.

"Referring to the discovery of this continent by 'the great nations of Europe,' the court acknowledged that those European conquerors would soon come into conflict over which nation could lay claim to which parcels of North America.

"The court defined the Discovery Doctrine, nowhere carved into the jurisprudence of the United States, as 'the principle that discovery gave title to the government by whose subjects or by whose authority it was made against all other European governments, which title might be consummated by possession.'

"The court continued, 'The exclusion of all other Europeans necessarily gave to the nation making the discovery the sole right of acquiring the soil from the natives and establishing settlements upon it.'

"Did you get that?" he asks. "In the eyes of the court, which had already commented that 'the character and religion of its inhabitants'—namely, the Indigenous people's culture and spirit—'afforded an apology for considering them as a people over whom the superior genius of Europe claim an ascendancy,' the British, French, and Spanish foot soldiers could claim property rights for their respective nations merely by being the first of their heritage to set foot on the land."

Joey interjects, "That is no different from concocting a law allowing invaders to break into your house, land their muddy boots in your foyer, and declare, 'This house now belongs to us. Your deed is worthless. But we'll let you stay here until we decide you must leave.'"

Joey's interest in the subject seems to have increased exponentially since he is now feeling supported in his beliefs by actual documented proof being expressed *and received* in a way his emotional railing never could.

Dr. Stone continues reading, "The court then discussed a series of various commissions, charters, and patents for land in the New World, dating back to 1496, and concluded, 'Thus has our whole country been granted by the Crown while in the occupation of the Indians,' and:

> *The United States, then, has unequivocally acceded to that great and broad rule by which its civilized inhabitants now hold this country. They hold and assert in themselves the title by which it was acquired. They maintain, as all others have maintained, that discovery gave an exclusive right to extinguish the Indian title of occupancy either by purchase or by conquest, and have also a right to such*

a degree of sovereignty as the circumstances of the people would allow them to exercise.

"In the court's reasoning, Britain's dominance became the United States' absolute right when the American colonists won their right to independence. So the same unadjudicated 'law,' the Discovery Doctrine, this sanctioned robbery, became the unquestionable province of the government of the United States.

"And instead of using its moral imperative to right the wrongs of the past, the court took the coward's way out. 'It is not for the courts of this country to question the validity of this title or to sustain one which is incompatible with it.'"

Dr. Stone reveals some heartfelt emotion through his next statement. "The language of the court regarding its opinion of Native Americans was so insulting and dismissive, I can hardly repeat it without gritting my teeth." He pauses, takes a couple of deep breaths, and continues. No matter how angry he got, he never raised his voice— but he never tried to hide his righteous indignation, either.

"The court actually said:

The tribes of Indians inhabiting this country were fierce savages whose occupation was war and whose subsistence was drawn chiefly from the forest. To leave them in possession of their country was to leave the country a wilderness; to govern them as a distinct people was impossible because...

"And here is where they really twist the knife—'they were as brave and as high spirited as they were fierce, and were ready to repel by arms every attempt on their independence.' What unbounded gall."

"Yes!" Joey has found an ally in Dr. Stone, one who can credibly articulate what he has been trying to tell the world for so long. They've formed a bond over their common disdain for these historical actions that were nothing less than criminal. "After taking away our rights to our land," Joey says, "to condescendingly pat us on the head with phony commendations. 'Why, you brave little savages, putting up such a good fight! Now behave, or we'll kick you off the land you've inhabited for thousands of years because everything you have belongs to us now.'"

Turning to the next page in the manuscript, Dr. Stone says, "You're right, Joey; that was the crux of that horrendous decision, and it has been affirmed in modern Supreme Court rulings more than a century and a half later."

He resumes reading. "In 1955, the Supreme Court decided Tee-Hit-Ton Indians v. United States, which involved the government-contracted taking of timber from a national forest in Alaska, on land occupied by the plaintiff Indian tribe.

"By a joint congressional resolution in 1947, the

Secretary of Agriculture was authorized to enter into such contracts 'notwithstanding any claim of possessory rights…based on aboriginal occupancy or title, whether claimed by native tribes, native villages, native individuals.'

"The court had to resolve the nature of the tribe's interest in the land. The Tlingits argued they needed to be compensated for the timber extracted from the land they occupied because, first, their ancestors continuously occupied and used the land 'from time immemorial'; second, when Russia took over Alaska, it did not interfere with the tribe's claim to the land, and third, Congress had confirmed and recognized their right to occupy the land permanently.

"The government argued the tribe only had the right to use the land at the government's will and was not entitled to compensation.

"The court held that Congress never explicitly granted 'the Indians any permanent rights in the lands of Alaska' but only allowed permissive occupation. The justification was based in significant part on the court's precedence validating the Discovery Doctrine, citing Johnson v. McIntosh. But the Tee-Hit-Ton court went further in its clarification and included the actual use of the land as a right exercised only by government permission.

"Further, on the issue of compensation, the court wrote,

'No case in the Court has ever held that taking of Indian title or use by Congress required compensation,' and then launched into some language as disingenuous as it was flowery:

> *The American people have compassion for the descendants of those Indians who were deprived of their homes and hunting grounds by the drive of civilization. They seek to have the Indians share the benefits of our society as citizens of this Nation. Generous provision has been willingly made to allow tribes to recover for wrongs.*

"Now get this clearly—'as a matter of grace, not because of legal liability.' Replace 'grace' with 'whim' or 'political expediency,' and you get a sense of how those words ring hollow in light of the government's broken promises and utter apathy toward the plight of all Indigenous people.

"The court held that the Tee-Hit-Ton people were not entitled to the compensation they sought and rationalized its decision with the court's traditional empty rhetoric:

> *Our conclusion does not uphold harshness as against tenderness toward the Indians, but it leaves with Congress, where it belongs, the policy of Indian gratuities for the termination of Indian occupancy of Government-owned land rather than making compensation for its value a rigid constitutional principle*

Dr. Diane Sharp

[referring to the Taking Clause of the Fifth Amendment].

"So you see, Indigenous people are specifically excluded from that supposed 'greatest document ever written by the hand of man,' the US Constitution, and frankly, the American dream. I'm saddened and angered and, perhaps more tragically, not surprised at all." All within earshot nod in silent agreement.

Ellen chimes in, "Even in the twenty-first century, the court has ruled against us, again based in part on the Discovery Doctrine."

"Sad but true." Dr. Stone continues reading, "Justice Ruth Bader Ginsberg wrote the court's opinion in the 2005 case of City of Sherrill v. Oneida Indian, a case emanating from New York State.

"Though the decision considered several other issues, in the first footnote, the court gives the nod to the Discovery Doctrine, citing it again without question of its validity. 'Under the "Doctrine of Discovery,"' says the footnote, 'fee title to the lands occupied by Indians when the colonists arrived became vested in the sovereign— first the discovering European nation and later the original States and the United States.'

"Frankly, I don't know whether the Discovery Doctrine, which essentially rewards invading nations for their brutal takeover of Indigenous populations, will ever be invalidated by the courts. But at least the last two cases I discussed had some dissenting opinions, so there may yet be hope."

Joey launches what will be his final diatribe of the day. "Our land was and *is* being stolen. You're all sitting in this very room on land that belongs to someone else. But, as some people like to say, 'That happens in war and conquests all the time. Arms were raised, and you lost the war.'

"Well, here's how I answer that statement. Here is the difference. Promises were made. Conditional treaties were written and agreed upon. We were forced onto reservations. To stop warring, our people made conditional agreements with your people. Just giving a parcel of land wasn't the agreement. Our leaders would never have agreed to learn your ways unless they knew their people would have everything they needed to survive.

"Read the treaties. Infrastructure was promised. Healthcare was promised. Adequate education for our people was promised. And none of it was delivered. You lied. You broke treaties. What good is a man if his word means nothing? I'll tell you what. He is less than a dog. A liar. Now exists not only poverty but a poverty of dreams.

"You go to your churches built on land taken by your lies. Women and children for centuries have suffered and are *still* suffering as a result of your lies. What kind of man does that? What kind of God does that?"

Joey realizes he is standing up, his finger pointed at the White crowd before him who, in his mind, represented all European conquerors and their descendants. He and I both realize he is talking to no one directly and yet to everyone. He is giving flight in the free air to his suffocating inner turmoil. His scathing look of disgust softens, and he calms down and sits back in his chair. It is as though he has been waiting for years to say these words to someone but never before had the chance. Even more, it is like the ancestors who suffered these atrocities in real time are, through him, speaking to their captors.

"We had a great way of life," he says in a muted, sulky voice. "We lived as one with the land, and it produced everything we needed to survive. You came through and purposely killed off millions of buffalo and sled dogs to drive us into starvation. It was cruel and far beyond the borders of what constitutes war. It was inhumane cruelty, and I," poking himself in the center of his chest, "will never forgive you."

Aunt Little Dance lets the silence go on just long enough so it doesn't seem she is dismissing Joey's pain or his position. She knows he is right. "But now," she speaks softly, "what do we do *now* to move forward? We have to know where we are going together."

"These men," she says to Joey, sweeping an inclusive

hand toward the White people congregated at the tables, "didn't do those things. But I understand you. You, like all of us, want to let people know what happened and how it impacts us and our people.

"It was a sin that shall be remembered in our blood forever. But we can work together to bring about change. Molly and many others like her showed us that. They cried for us when they saw the living conditions and the hopeless looks on the faces of our youth. But more importantly she and others are crying *with* us and desiring to heal *with* us and make a plan to move forward *with* us.

"It is true that the work to heal our people must be done by our people. But we cannot continue to hold White people accountable if we are not willing to give them an opportunity to come and help us. We blame them for not providing what we needed to survive after being forced onto reservations, yet we refuse their help now when it is offered with pure hearts.

"Nephew, I have been working with our youth for longer than you've been alive. I have seen the shift in the hearts of Wasicu, the White outsiders who have come to help. It is a different, greater purity now than I have seen in many years. Creator is placing people in our path who are pure in heart, want to help, and have the means to do so. Molly and her teams also showed us that. Some still have a lot to learn, but we must now take the position as teachers. Their schools have failed them in the effort to hide what their ancestors did, yet every generation has gotten closer and closer to the truth.

"We must teach them now what Creator has assigned us to teach them so they can continue in this direction of knowing the truth, for it is only in the knowledge of the truth of history that they can actually do something meaningful today.

"Otherwise, it is help based on faulty information, and it will miss the mark every time. A helping program is only effective if they truly know the need and all of the areas of our way of life and our psyche that will be impacted by their help. We cannot hold people accountable for what we are not willing to teach them, and that requires conversation from a perspective of understanding.

"My dear nephew, you're a teacher. Would you give a test to your students having not first taught them the lesson? We know truth as it was presented to us by our ancestors who lived it. Their truth was tainted by history books that depicted White people only as heroes and hid the shame of their actions with stories filled with inaccuracies that painted them as the heroes or the victims but never as the villains. We must also be honest with ourselves to know that we, as much as we can justify it, acted villainously at times too. We were not always the hero. No man is. I hear you. I am angry, too, but not at the people who are now reaching out to help.

"We have to focus on what we do with our time now. Time is short, too short to operate in hate, anger, and bitterness anymore. Let's change the trajectory of our relationship with the White man and the Christian church. Let's teach now rather than accuse. I promise you they don't know what really happened, but they want to know." Catching herself, she amends her assessment. "Some want to know. I see purity in their eyes when they ask me questions.

"Help them to know, and then you can learn to benefit from their ideas and knowledge. It is wisdom to expand your resources by allowing others to contribute their wisdom. How much more could we do for our people with a larger circle of people to help us? Do not let bitterness rob your people of all you can do for them. If you do, you are to blame."

Joey sits quietly, absorbing Auntie's sage advice, and then softly addresses her with the respect one gives to an elder. "Auntie, I understand that some want to help; I really do. But am I to teach them an entire country's history? Is that my responsibility? I've seen their 'helping programs' do more harm than good."

"Start by teaching them of you," Auntie says gently, pointing to the center of his chest. "Talk openly about who you are and what is important to you. We have to continue to be available to tell our own narratives. If we teach these groups what is important to us, then they are

Dr. Diane Sharp

smart enough to formulate their programs around that. Not all of them want to change us to be just like them. These people"—motioning to the group—"are smart enough to know that our ways are important to us and not to make a plan to help in any manner that would damage our way of life.

"Some people know how to help in a manner that works within our culture, and some don't. That's where your responsibility starts. You have to teach them what those cultural ways are so they can take them into account when planning their help."

Sheila excitedly asks, "So how can I help? What can I do?"

Deanna offers up, "Well, first we need to make sure we don't take part in placing any more stones on top of this faulty foundation of the Doctrine of Discovery that led to systemic racism. I imagine that will look a little different for each of us as we operationalize this new information. For me, I am going to study everything I can about the history of this doctrine and teach my friends and family the truth of our nation's history."

Though Joey seems to acknowledge Deanna's sincerity, his facial expression and body language reveal equal parts of anger, frustration, and defiance. "My culture is mine. When the colonists came in—and to be honest, even now—there was a drive to remove my culture from me. They even said it themselves that their desire was to kill the Indian and save the man. What do you think that meant? To take away everything that made me Lakota. And now it's like you want me to hand them my culture on a platter to misappropriate and steal. It is not theirs to know; it is mine. Their plan didn't work. We are still here. We are here with our culture. They failed to kill it.

"My blood remembers the attempt to steal my culture, and I will hold on to it with everything I have. I must keep my heritage at all costs. Sometimes I feel like that's all I have left that they didn't take. They took our land and our way of life, but they couldn't take our culture.

"I don't want them at my sun dances or using my sweat lodges as though they are nothing more than saunas. I hate to see all these people burning sage or smudging without any knowledge of what it represents, misappropriating *my* culture, and using the teepee like it's just another tent. Those are valuable pieces of my culture, and that is all I have left. They brought their God and their ways and tried to force us to believe in Him by ripping away what we had been doing for generations. It wasn't right. I don't want a God like that. A good God would never—" Joey's gaze drifts off as he slides his hands into his pockets to signify he is done. Auntie is getting through, but he just isn't ready to let go. *That's okay, Joey. It will take time.*

Not one to waste an opportunity to exploit existing drama, Patrick launches his own rhetorical volley.

Dr. Diane Sharp

"Realistically, what do you want me to do now? Move out of my house and give my land to someone else? To who? And go where?

"I got up every day, worked hard, and went without to save my hard-earned money to be able to buy that home. It wasn't given to me. It wasn't privilege that afforded that to me.

"Look, I acknowledge that the lands were taken by deception; I do. Extorted by threats and stolen by savage acts. I see that. My ancestors sold land that wasn't theirs to sell, and now I have some of it. I guess that's where the generational privilege comes in. I had the opportunity to buy something that shouldn't have been available in the first place.

"But it is what it is now, and I should be allowed to live the life I've built for myself—regardless of what my long-dead ancestors did, right?"

Terry quietly clears his throat, and as I look at him, I notice an almost majestic softness in his demeanor beyond what I've ever seen before. I look deep into his eyes and swear I see the flicker of a glorious epiphany light up his soul. I may be late to the game, but I'll admit now that I've never been prouder to be known as his sister.

In a voice marked with a kindness that turned heads, he tells Patrick, "Yes, we are privileged, and we are called by the God of all of us"—he motions to everyone in the group—"to be good stewards. He gave you the ability to acquire everything you have. Now it's your turn—our turn—to give back to God by using those resources to help lift others to a new hope and a new life.

"As someone once wrote," he said, careful not to telegraph that he was going to quote a Bible passage, "'If possible, so far as it depends on you, live peaceably with all.'[1] Maybe that starts with talking like we're doing now and investing a bit of our time and money to help the cause of healing and reconciliation between two nations Christ died for."

Dr. Stone nods his agreement and leans toward Joey. "It hurts my heart to hear that what those people did left such a scar on your opinion of God and who He is. I am sorry for that. They tragically squandered an opportunity for divine ambassadorship. But if I may, I'd like to tell you who He was then and who He is now. He never changes."

Now it was Dr. Stone's turn to speak to one person and yet to all Indigenous peoples.

"He was always your God. He revealed Himself to your ancestors through all created things and all creatures of the earth, through nature itself and its operation. The way animals, plants, and flowers all grow, have seasons, and relate to one another all reveal His attributes. He has revealed Himself through the plants, which feed from the sun, and through the moon when it lights up the night as flowers close up to rest, in the tides of the sea and flow of the rivers whose edges stop exactly where He commands. So many Lakota virtues and values are paralleled in the Bible.

"All that is visible reveals enough of all that is invisible in Him for man to gain an initial understanding of who He is. God was using nature to develop a relationship between you and Him. And that occurred long before any colonists took it upon themselves to bestow their perverted form of Christianity to this land. They were, in fact, an interruption in the cultivation of this relationship sent by the enemy of your soul, the devil.

"God was already revealing Himself to your ancestors through dreams, through nature, and through visions. He has always been speaking directly to you through no self-appointed intermediary. The Great I Am, Creator of all things, is now and always was your God—yours for the choosing. He is not 'someone else's God' to be forced upon you and accepted.

"God will never force Himself on anyone. He loves us to a point we can no longer deny that He is exactly who He says He is. He has always been living among you, beckoning you into right relationship with Him. He didn't need to be 'carried' to you by anyone. He is not a 'thing' to be owned and distributed at the will of man. He cannot be contained!

"King Solomon was chosen to build a great palace for God, a place to burn offerings to Him. It was referred to as a 'house' for God. Solomon acknowledged that, yes, he was building a great house for God, but who was he to build that house? He declared that even the heaven and the heaven of heavens could not contain Him! No man can box God up to give to another. They can only make the introduction by presenting the truth of the gospel. God has to reveal Himself to you and personally beckon you to salvation and into right relationship with Him. I believe He is doing that now.

"Who is this 'He'? He is God the Father (Creator God), Jesus Christ the Son, and the Person of the Holy Spirit. God has always been and will always be. He is the Alpha and the Omega, which means He is the beginning and the end. These three persons in one have been since the beginning and have never been limited to a geographic location, religion, or culture. God refers to Himself as 'We' in the beginning book of the Bible when He discussed creating the world. It is impossible to separate these three from one another. A saving relationship with Jesus, making Him your Lord, is a must to go to heaven.

"He was not the property of the colonists any more than He is only the White man's Jesus today. This is the day to take back what has always been yours: direct access to the Creator and His Son and the Person of the Holy Spirit, who have always been yours to accept. Take the opportunity back as though those 'Christians' had never come and invaded. Detach the association of Jesus from the colonists. He was never attached to their agenda in the first place. Your ancestors met the empire, not the man.

"There is an enemy of our soul who seeks to destroy us. He is not a race of people but an evil being who was cast out of heaven. He is deathly afraid that you will find out who you are in the eyes of God and the authority you will have once you accept Christ. He is afraid of the power that will ensue as you operate in the authority of God through Jesus—especially people as strong, loyal, and enduring as you. Once you find out who you are in the eyes of your loving God, in Christ, there will be no stopping you—and the enemy knows it.

"I implore you: If you don't know Him, give Him a chance. You can even ask Him and say, 'Jesus, if You're real, show me…' He's up to the challenge. He understands the history, and He, more than anyone, wants to turn this thing around. He's beckoning those who don't know Him into a relationship with Him, saying, 'Come. Please. Come unto me. My yoke is easy. My burden is light.' Salvation depends on it. Living forever depends on it. He's the only way, the truth, and the light. Jesus is very, very real.

"If the devil can keep you hating the idea of Jesus as though Jesus is attached to one particular race of people, the enemy has won. That enemy will continue his reign in your lands, continue to torment your youth with thoughts of suicide, and do all he can to see that your people live in a despair he thoroughly enjoys. No one can defeat you. You're still here. Choose your Jesus today, the One who never breaks a promise. He has always been yours."

As both Dr. Stone and Joey sit back, the crowd of onlookers and the circle remains still and silent, somehow knowing there is nothing else to be said here but so much more yet to talk about.

Joey lets out a deep breath, not in defeat but rather in contemplation. I see hope. I see a conversation started that won't be totally resolved today but started. I see a softening in Joey's eyes. In all of their eyes toward one another.

****

CHAPTER 7

I remember when one of the teams to the reservation was given a tour of the site of the Wounded Knee Massacre. Our Lakota tour guide told us the history of the massacre and the deep feelings of his own heart pertaining to the relationship between Christians and his people.

He raised his soft yet confident storytelling voice only loud enough to be heard over the blowing prairie winds. His eyes expressed his desire for our team to grasp his words and take them home to share with our circles. He said, "We need our people to come back to the reservation and help us, and we need those who have left to get educated and trained to return. God knows where they are, and He will send them home."

He had no idea of my story (though my team members did) about my having been sent back home to the reservation. The team all shifted their gaze toward me as though I were somehow one living answer to his prayer, one Lakota soul who had returned home, making a difference for her people. I never quite felt like I did this in my life, but maybe in my death…

****

CHAPTER 8

I survey the circle and arc of chairs. Everyone is silent, motionless, and deep in thought. Wave upon wave of joy sweeps over me as I contemplate the levels of meaning underlying this scene.

Everyone spoke their heart.

Everyone listened.

Though the conversation got a little contentious at times, everyone ended up contemplating issues bigger than they are.

Everyone was spent. They had voiced their say.

The dialogue, and hopefully the reconciliation, had begun.

This is all I ever really wanted. Maybe my feeble efforts did make a difference. Now I am ready to travel to the next place God has for me.

But first, if I could, I would call the monument company and ask them to change the epitaph on my headstone to read, "Left it better than I found it."

****

CHAPTER 9

The microphone screeches from the stage one last time as the all-clear is given for everyone to return to the worship center to gather their wet belongings. The funeral is over, and my body is being taken out of the building and will soon be headed to the cemetery.

The circle stands, and everyone shakes hands with a quiet humility that feels like they have all learned a bit more about themselves than they have about each other. The crowd rocks back and forth on their feet as they slowly make their way to the bottleneck at the door to make their escape.

I stay behind for a bit. I guess part of me wants to linger, while the greater part of me is ready to go on to my reward. The remnants of spaghetti don't look near as pretty as the original dish. I, of course, didn't eat any, but the smell is still wondrous.

The room is empty of the people I loved and who loved

me in return. I imagine this is the last time I will see them—well, up close and personal. I'm not sure what my view will be in the next phase of my eternal existence.

Aunt Little Dance and Ellen stop near the hearse and dig something out of her tote. As the bright colors are unveiled, I recognize it immediately. It's a star quilt! I always wanted to be given one of those quilts, which held a measure of honor, love, and for me, belonging. I had always felt as though being presented with a star quilt would somehow make me a little more Lakota.

They walk in reverent silence to my casket, now being loaded into the hearse. They drape my casket with the quilt and whisper the Lakota name I'd always longed for…

RECONCILIATION CALLS TO ACTION

1. Support efforts to empower Indigenous community leaders in their quest to bring about change.
2. Commit resources, time (prayer, acts of service), treasure (money, supplies).
3. Use your personal sphere of influence to engage in helping relationships (go on a service trip!).
4. Educate yourself and those around you about the real history and current context.
5. Press lawmakers at the local, state, and national levels to engage in reconciliatory and social justice efforts (renunciation of the Doctrine of Discovery).
6. Personally renounce the Doctrine of Discovery and residential school atrocities. Break that covenant!
7. Do no harm. Change negative thought patterns toward other people groups.
8. Start with one act...start today.
9. Wopila.

ENDNOTES

1 Romans 12:18.

Scan the QR code to see how you can partner with the Indigenous Community Empowerment Network.

About | Indigenous Community Empowerment

www.icenetwork.org

Printed in the USA
CPSIA information can be obtained
at www.ICGtesting.com
LVHW012334090823
754782LV00001B/1